HAL•LEONARD
INSTRUMENTAL PLAY-ALONG

AUDIO ACCESS INCLUDED

PLAYBACK+
Speed • Pitch • Balance • Loop

TROMBONE

THE BEATLES

Cover Photo: Fiona Adams/Getty

To access audio visit:
www.halleonard.com/mylibrary

Enter Code
8329-7043-8728-1767

Audio Arrangements by Peter Deneff

ISBN 978-1-4950-9072-1

HAL•LEONARD®

7777 W. BLUEMOUND RD. P.O. BOX 13819 MILWAUKEE, WI 53213

In Australia Contact:
Hal Leonard Australia Pty. Ltd.
4 Lentara Court
Cheltenham, Victoria, 3192 Australia
Email: ausadmin@halleonard.com.au

Visit Hal Leonard Online at
www.halleonard.com

ALL YOU NEED IS LOVE

TROMBONE

Words and Music by JOHN LENNON
and PAUL McCARTNEY

BLACKBIRD

TROMBONE

Words and Music by JOHN LENNON
and PAUL McCARTNEY

DAY TRIPPER

TROMBONE

Words and Music by JOHN LENNON
and PAUL McCARTNEY

ELEANOR RIGBY

TROMBONE

Words and Music by JOHN LENNON
and PAUL McCARTNEY

GET BACK

TROMBONE

Words and Music by JOHN LENNON
and PAUL McCARTNEY

HERE, THERE AND EVERYWHERE

TROMBONE

Words and Music by JOHN LENNON
and PAUL McCARTNEY

HEY JUDE

TROMBONE

Words and Music by JOHN LENNON
and PAUL McCARTNEY

I WILL

TROMBONE

Words and Music by JOHN LENNON
and PAUL McCARTNEY

LET IT BE

TROMBONE

Words and Music by JOHN LENNON
and PAUL McCARTNEY

LUCY IN THE SKY WITH DIAMONDS

TROMBONE

Words and Music by JOHN LENNON
and PAUL McCARTNEY

OB-LA-DI, OB-LA-DA

TROMBONE

Words and Music by JOHN LENNON
and PAUL McCARTNEY

PENNY LANE

TROMBONE

Words and Music by JOHN LENNON
and PAUL McCARTNEY

SOMETHING

TROMBONE

Words and Music by
GEORGE HARRISON

TICKET TO RIDE

TROMBONE

Words and Music by JOHN LENNON
and PAUL McCARTNEY

YESTERDAY

TROMBONE

Words and Music by JOHN LENNON
and PAUL McCARTNEY